YOUR KNOWLEDGE H

Verena Schörkhuber

Metafiction in J.M. Coetzee's 'Foe'

GRIN Verlag

Bibliografische Information der Deutschen Nationalbibliothek:

Die Deutsche Bibliothek verzeichnet diese Publikation in der Deutschen National-
bibliografie; detaillierte bibliografische Daten sind im Internet über http://dnb.d-
nb.de/ abrufbar.

Imprint:

Copyright © 2006 GRIN Verlag GmbH
Druck und Bindung: Books on Demand GmbH, Norderstedt Germany
ISBN: 978-3-638-76653-1

This book at GRIN:

http://www.grin.com/en/e-book/59730/metafiction-in-j-m-coetzee-s-foe

GRIN - Your knowledge has value

Der GRIN Verlag publiziert seit 1998 wissenschaftliche Arbeiten von Studenten, Hochschullehrern und anderen Akademikern als eBook und gedrucktes Buch. Die Verlagswebsite www.grin.com ist die ideale Plattform zur Veröffentlichung von Hausarbeiten, Abschlussarbeiten, wissenschaftlichen Aufsätzen, Dissertationen und Fachbüchern.

Visit us on the internet:

http://www.grin.com/

http://www.facebook.com/grincom

http://www.twitter.com/grin_com

PS Literature: Introductory Seminar (304)

The Post-Modern Condition

Summer Semester 2006

Metafiction
in J. M. Coetzee's *Foe*

Verena Schörkhuber

New Curriculum

Table of contents

1. Introduction

The main aim of this paper is to discuss metafiction in J. M. Coetzee's *Foe* (1986)[1], which is a rewriting of Daniel Defoe's literary classic *Robinson Crusoe* (1719)[2]. As a fiction about the origins of *Crusoe*, Coetzee's *Foe* addresses the problematic issues in *Crusoe*, in particular the absence of female characters and Friday's inefficacy to represent an independent personality, by 'exposing the silences in the original and giving them voice' (James, 6). Defoe, obscured behind the persona of the narrator in *Crusoe*, is '[forced] [...] out into the open and [exposed] [...] for what he is, the "foe", Mr Foe, the giver of false witness' (Burnett, 244).[3]

As a discussion of *Foe* inevitably raises questions of how far Coetzee was using *Crusoe* to explore the South African context, I shall deal not only with the position of Coetzee and his texts as discussed by various critics, but also with the intersection of postcolonialism and postmodernism in his works and suggest that even though there might be a perception of the 'marginalisation of ethical discourse [...] [as] a result of the rise of poststructuralist theory' (Yeoh, 1), Coetzee has made a counter-argument, '[insisting] on the inescapability of ethics' (Yeoh, 2) despite his privileging of textuality. Subsequently this paper shall give (a) definition(s) of a dominant subject of postmodern fiction, namely metafiction, and consider the origins of this term and its general functions.[4] On the basis of my personal reading of *Foe* and several secondary sources drawn upon, I will finally take a rather detailed look at metafiction and, related to this, the discourse of power in Coetzee's deconstruction of the Crusoe myth.

---

[1] All references to *Foe* (henceforth abbreviated as *F*) are to the Penguin edition (Harmondsworth: Penguin, 1987)
[2] Due to the limitations of a paper like this, 'intertextuality' can unfortunately not be addressed.
[3] By uncovering Defoe to be Foe, Coetzee reminds the reader that Daniel Defoe adopted the prefix 'de' in his middle age, obscuring his name's signification in English. Cf. Burnett, 245.
[4] As a detailed discussion of these and various other aspects would go beyond the scope of a paper like this, the aim of the section entitled 'Metafiction' will be merely to provide an introduction to and outline of metafiction.

2. Coetzee's place in contemporary writing

2.1 The position of Coetzee and his texts

As a white South African, Coetzee writes from the position of a member of the dominant group and has thus access to a power which is denied to the majority of Native Americans. While some critics argue that his fiction evades its responsibility towards South Africa by eliding its immediate political reality during and in the wake of apartheid, others read his texts as allegories of the contemporary South African situation, dramatising 'the complicity of colonial settler narratives with exploitative politico-historical processes' (Wright, 118, quoted Egerer, 95). Others of a more deconstructive interest see Coetzee's main concern in language, with his writing being one that 'interrogates, challenges, casts into doubt' (Olsen, 47, quoted in Egerer, 95). Yet another group of critics reconcile self-reflexive elements with a contextual reading, arguing that while texts like *Foe* can be read as an 'allegory of the creative process' (Splendore, 58), they also '[lay] bare the ambiguity of the social drama' (Splendore, 60).

What emerges from these critical perspectives is that within a materialist agenda, Coetzee's writing is seen as 'marginal' in the sense of not taking an explicit stand against South-African socio-historical conditions; seen as South-African postmodern writing, it is also 'marginal' to the tradition of postmodernism insofar as the majority of postmodern texts are associated with South- and Anglo-America.[5] Reading Attwell's comments in Coetzee's *Doubling the Point* confirms once more the impossibility of (self-)positioning. Distancing himself from a mode of thinking which constructs a new opposition between 'exhausted metropolis and vigorous periphery' (202), Coetzee rejects these classifications, privileging instead the tensions resulting from 'a will to remain in crisis' (337).

---

[5] Cf. Egerer, 96

2.2 The intersection of postcolonialism and postmodernism

Coetzee's novels occupy a special place not only in South African literature, but also in the development of the twentieth-century novel in general, because he is 'the first South African writer to produce overtly self-conscious fictions drawing explicitly on international postmodernism', importing 'contemporary Western preoccupations which produce a stress on textuality to a degree not previously seen in his country's literature' (Head, 1). Newman proceeds upon the assumption that 'postcolonial fictions are themselves "theoretical" in their counter-readings of master narratives', and 'have in themselves the interpretive power which dominant theoretical practice usually grants to the literary critic' (193).

A major Coetzee critic, Attwell's assertion that Coetzee's first six novels 'constitute a form of postmodern metafiction' (*Politics*, 1) has become a pioneering path taken by many other critics. Attwell, denying the general reading of postmodernism as anti-historical, describes Coetzee's novels as 'situational metafiction, with a particular relation to the cultural and political discourses of South Africa in the 1970s and 1980s' (*Politics*, 3). In Coetzee's most obviously metafictional text *Foe*, a 'self-referential fiction that constantly highlights its own unreliability'[6] (Gallagher, 44), political and literary rewritings go hand in hand: the 'imperialist' author Foe appropriates the story of the colonial subject and, in a form of gender apartheid, eliminates the female from the adventure genre.[7] In *Foe* the postmodern and the postcolonial thus co-exist as ideological allies, enabling Coetzee to adopt 'postmodern strategies […] for postcolonial purposes' (Begam, 112, quoted in Lin, 123).

---

[6] The effect of this self-consciousness should, however, not be overstated, as it does not present unreliability to disturb the surface reading experience in the way some postmodernist works do. Cf. Head, 9.
[7] Cf. Newman, 96

Paradoxically it is this self-consciousness which makes the political point. Whereas the British writer can merge with his or her society, since that society has, in a sense, appropriated reality, the postcolonial writer must avoid any loss of self-awareness. Postcolonial writers are therefore often at their politically sharpest, when they are also at their most 'literary'. (Newman, 4)

3. Metafiction
3.1 Origins of the term and its function today

To begin with, the development of the term 'metalanguage' is commonly ascribed to the linguist Louis Hjelmslev, according to whom metalanguage, instead of referring to non-linguistic events, situations, or objects in the world, refers to another language[8]. Clearly Saussure's distinction between a sign's signifier and signified is relevant here: a metalanguage is a language which functions as a signifier to another language, which becomes its signified. The term 'metafiction' as a novel's self-reflexive tendency itself is generally attributed to *Fiction and the figures of life* by the American critic and self-conscious novelist William Gass in 1970.[9]

Metafictional practice has become particularly prominent in the fiction of the last twenty years, reflecting on the breakdown of traditional values in a world consisting no longer of eternal verities (Waugh, 7). Attempting to defend twentieth century metafiction, theorists cite older classic works such as Cervantes' *Don Quixote* (1605), Shakespeare's *Hamlet* (around 1600) and Austen's *Northanger Abbey* (1817) as demonstrating metafictional tendency. While critics suggest that metafiction illustrates the death or 'exhaustion' of the novel as a genre, its advocates regard it as signalling the novel's rebirth:

---

[8] Cf. Hjelmslev, Louis. *Prolegomena to a Theory of Language*. Madison: Wisconsin, 1961.
[9] Cf. Ommundsen, 14

[F]ar from 'dying', the novel has reached a mature recognition of its existence as *writing*, which can only ensure its continued viability in [...] a contemporary world which is similarly beginning to gain awareness of precisely how its values and practices are constructed [...]. (Waugh, 19)

Already in 1975, Federman called for 'a fiction [trying] to explore the possibilities of fiction' (7) and envisaged the future novel as 'a kind of writing [...] whose shape will be an interrogation [...] of what it really is: an illusion (a fiction), just as life is an illusion (a fiction)' (11). Similarly, for Quendler, 'the plea for an innovation of fiction is preceded by a critically metafictional divestment of conventions of narrative fiction [...] to re-describe the relations between [...] fictions and reality' (39).

3.2 Definition(s) and forms of metafiction

According to Hutcheon, metafiction is 'fiction about fiction – that is, fiction that includes within itself a commentary on its own narrative and/or linguistic identity' (1). Waugh sees metafiction as a 'tendency inherent to all novels' (2) and defines it as 'a term given to fictional writing which self-consciously and systematically draws attention to its status as an artefact' (2) in order to raise questions about the problematic relationship between fiction and reality. Writers whom one might refer to as broadly 'metafictional' are concerned with providing a critique of their own methods of constructing their literary fictional texts by '[exploring] a *theory* of fiction through the *practice* of writing fiction' (2). These scholars thus emphasise the ways in which metafictional texts manifest their preoccupation with texts: the relationships between constructing, reading and interpreting texts and reality.

Waugh identifies three types of metafiction. Fowles' subversion of the 'omniscient narrator' in *The French Lieutenant's Woman* (1969) belongs to the first type, which upsets a particular convention of the novel. Within the second type, one can find works which, 'often in the form of a parody, comment on a specific work or fictional mode'[10] (4). The third type, exemplified by Richard Brautigan's *Trout Fishing in America* (1967), are less overtly metafictional novels which still display 'meta' features in creating 'alternative linguistic structures or fictions which merely *imply* the old forms', and which '[encourage] the reader to draw on his or her

---

[10] For instance, Fowles' *Mantissa* (1982) is a self-reflexive novel on the self-reflexive novel.

knowledge of traditional literary conventions when struggling to construct a meaning for the new text' (4). Needless to say, Coetzee's *Foe* needs to be examined under this light.

Lyotard states that '[s]implifying to the extreme, I define *postmodern* as incredulity towards metanarratives' (xxiv), resulting in the writer 'working without rules in order to formulate the rules of what *will have been done*' (83). Due to the lack of rules which the now extinct 'master narratives' once supplied, the postmodern writer is a rule maker out of necessity.[11] His metafictional work thus 'either directly examines its own construction as it proceeds or [...] comments or speculates about the forms and language of previous fictions' (McCaffery, 16). Wolf mentions the term 'critical metafiction', i.e. the critical exposure of fictitiousness within a fictional text, in this context, with 'fictitiousness' including both the ontological status of fiction (i.e. its fictionality) and the referential deviation from pragmatic or reporting discourse (i.e. its fictivity). He also introduces the terms 'Eigen-', 'Fremd-' and 'Allgemeinmetafiktion' to indicate whether metafiction occurs with reference to its own text, to other specific pre-texts, or to literature in general.[12]

To conclude, Ommundsen warns that postmodernism is 'a category so complex and disputed that its relationship to metafiction cannot be precisely defined' (14). The majority of theorists, however, agree that metafiction cannot be classified as a genre nor as a definite mode of postmodern fiction, but rather as 'a self-reflexivity prompted by the author's awareness of the theory underlying the construction of fictional works' (Waugh, 2):

> [T]he lowest common denominator of metafiction is simultaneously to create a fiction and to make a statement about the creation of that fiction. The two processes are held together in a formal tension which breaks down the distinctions between 'creation' and 'criticism' and merges them into the concepts of 'interpretation' and 'deconstruction.' (Waugh, 6)

---

[11] Cf. Scott, 15
[12] Cf. Wolf, 38ff.

4. Metafiction and the discourse of power in *Foe*

4.1 An overview

As its title already suggests, *Foe* is a novel about enmity, about how 'the voice of the elite culture of patriarchal power', namely (De)Foe, 'comes to marginalise the vernacular voice of the woman, the Other of gender, and to "drown" out completely the voice of the racial Other, Friday' (Burnett, 245). Unsurprisingly, concepts of power are closely linked to the post-modern reflection on language and text. Thereby, 'the focus on language in *Foe* is less concerned with intertextual possibilities [...] than with a very extensive metafictional discourse' (Corcoran, 257).

The larger part of the novel consists of a memoir and several letters written by the newly returned castaway Susan Barton to Foe:

> [Q]uotation marks before each of her paragraphs [remind] us constantly that this is not the mysterious immaterial language most fiction uses as its medium, nor even a representation of speech, but a representation *in* writing *of* writing. And it is presented not as a simple day-to-day record of experience, as in a novel of letters or diary-entries, but for the explicit purpose of proffering a narrative [...] for insertion into the canon of published English texts. (Attridge, 73)

After the 'narrative' proper, i.e. Susan's account of her island story, in the first section, sections two and three show Susan's struggle against being written out of her own novel; to assess how much rewriting her story requires to render it fit for the developing bourgeois canon of the early eighteenth century we need only turn to Defoe's novel.[13]

4.2 Part I

When reading *Foe*, what might strike the reader first is Coetzee's spelling of 'Cruso'. Extending the Derridean concept of 'différance', whose potency derives from a 'silent lapse in spelling' (Derrida, *Margins*, 3), Coetzee replaces the 'e' in 'Crusoe' not with another letter, but with the absence of a letter; this silence cannot be heard, only written or read, but makes

---

[13] Cf. Attridge, 77-78.

all the difference: 'the movement of difference, as [...] that which differentiates, is the common root of all oppositional concepts that mark our language [...].' (Derrida, *Positions*, 8) The lack of an 'e' can thus be read as a distinguishing mark from the urtext's Crusoe; and indeed, throughout the whole novel, the character of Cruso does not follow the novelistic tradition of castaway stories Susan is strangely familiar with[14], which signals her metafictional status; for instance, when she arrives on the island, she reflects on the comparison of fictional stereotypes to 'reality', a reality which is itself a fictional creation:[15]

> For readers reared on travellers' tales, the words *desert isle* may conjure up a place of soft sands and shady trees where brooks run to quench the castaway's thirst and ripe fruit falls into his hand [...]. But the island on which I was cast away was quite another place: a great rocky hill with a flat top, rising sharply from the sea [...]. (*F*, 7)

'This comparison between an ostensibly fictional version of reality', namely *Robinson Crusoe* as a real novel, 'and events purported to be taking place in the supposedly real world, is omnipresent in the novel' (Corcoran, 258). However, more often than not, the comparison between 'fact' and 'fiction' is 'blurred', resulting in confusion. This is stated by Susan, when she challenges Cruso's capacity to distinguish 'truth' from 'fancy':

> I would gladly now recount to you the history of this singular Cruso [...]. But the stories he told me were so various, and so hard to reconcile with another, that I was more and more driven to conclude age and isolation had taken their toll on his memory, and he no longer knew for sure what was truth, what fancy. (*F*, 11-12)

Contrasting Cruso's indifference to language and having no understanding for his refusal to keep a journal, Susan argues for what might be a 'theory of fiction' concerned with the realistic fictional effect so as to guarantee a story's substantiality. To her mind, writing down events is a way of 'endowing them with the status of reality which they would otherwise never achieve' (Corcoran, 258):

---

[14] Cf. Egerer, 114
[15] Cf. Corcoran, 257

[S]een from too remote a vantage, life begins to lose its particularity. All shipwrecks become the same shipwreck, all castaways the same castaway [...]. The truth that makes your story yours alone, that sets you apart from the old mariner by the fireside spinning yarns of sea-monsters and mermaids, resides in a thousand touches which [...] will one day persuade your countrymen that it is all true, every word [...]. (*F*, 18)

When Susan arrives on the island, she tells Cruso what had happened to her and thus enters the realm of story-telling; however, hers and Cruso's views of the limits of their stories differ:

When I spoke of England and of all the things I intended to see and do when I was rescued, he seemed not to hear me. It was as though he wished his story to begin with his arrival on the island, and mine to begin with my arrival, and the story of us together to end on the island too. (*F*, 34)

Throughout the whole novel, the metafictional discourse is closely related to an investigation of power-relationships; for example, Friday's tongue might have been cut out by the slavers because 'they wanted to prevent him from ever telling his story' (*F*, 23). The island episode ends with the rescue of Susan and, though reluctant, Cruso and Friday, with Susan's victory '[being] tantamount to a usurping of the role of the protagonists, Cruso and Friday, in their own narrative' (Corcoran, 260).

4.3 Parts II and III

In the subsequent narrative of events, which has already been reported in the first section, Susan longs for Foe to write down her story: 'Return to me the substance I have lost, Mr Foe' (*F*, 51). Clearly, Susan fears that she lacks substance as an individual until her story is written as a legitimated narrative, because she, like all fictional characters, is created by the writing of the story[16]. A struggle over who is in control of the narrative ensues; while Susan insists that her searching for her daughter is not part of her story, Foe wants to shape her story according to his own design[17]:

---

[16] In fact, Susan does have an aura of insubstantiality, precisely because of the canonic power of Defoe's novel.
[17] Cf. Corcoran, 261-262

We [...] have five parts in all: the loss of the daughter; the quest for the daughter in Brazil; abandonment of the quest, and the adventure of the island; assumption of the quest by the daughter; and reunion of the daughter with her mother. It is thus that we make up a book: [...] beginning, then middle, then end. (*F*, 117)

Foe threatens Susan not only by determining the form, but also the content of her story. He is much more attracted to Susan's own story before the period on the island, involving her lost daughter, whose reality, within the fictional world, is thrown into question by the reader's awareness that her story is told in another of Defoe's novels, *Roxana*. The text does not answer whether her daughter is 'a ghost – a fictional potentiality never brought to fruition – or a substantial being which has won a place in the narrative' (Corcoran, 264). Susan clearly sees that the author is a 'creator' of both fiction and reality, because for her, the daughter is 'father-born' (*F*, 91), called into life by Foe. However, after her long debate with Foe, she seems to move towards his position, stating that there are no distinctions to be made between characters invented by an author and individuals with an independent reality.[18] In answer to his question about the substantiality of the girl, she concedes: 'she is substantial, as my daughter is substantial, and I am substantial [...]. [W]e are all substantial, we are all in the same world'[19] (*F*, 152). Foe might then be read 'as an exploration of a fact that is central to the processes of canonization', namely that 'human experience seems lacking in substance and significance if it is not represented (to oneself and to others) in culturally validated narrative forms' (Attridge, 80).

When confronted with the daughter and her maid, Susan expresses doubts about her identity: '[b]ut if these women are creatures of yours, visiting me at your instruction, speaking words you have prepared for them, then who am I and who indeed are you? [...] Who is speaking me? Am I a phantom too? To what order do I belong?' (*F*, 133). The self-conscious uncertainty of the character and the hint to fictionality could not be more obvious. But it is not only Susan who, as a character of the novel, dwells on her role as the author's creation; she also draws Foe into this philosophical speculation on (in)substantiality. Foe, describing his own 'maze of doubting' (*F*, 135), replies that 'all of us [have] been called into the world from a different order [...] by a conjurer unknown to us' (*F*, 135). We as readers of course know that their 'conjurer' is Coetzee.

---

[18] Attridge, 79
[19] Needless to say, for us as readers, this is the world created by Coetzee's novel.

The gender-reversal Susan seeks in her wish to be 'father to my story' (*F*, 123) is twice referred to in the context of literary creation; namely when she sees Foe as a 'wife' who she has attempted to impregnate with the seed of her story[20], and when she tries to reverse the traditional role of author and muse: 'I wish that there were such a being as a man-Muse, a youthful god who visited authoresses in the night and made their pens flow.' (*F*, 126)

After Susan's efforts to bring Friday to speech have failed, Foe suggests to teach him writing; Susan, however, wonders: '[h]ow can he write if he cannot speak?' (*F*, 142). In contrast to Susan, Foe does not assume that Friday can have no narrative voice and contradicts Susan's conventional belief that '[l]etters are the mirror of words' with the poststructuralist insight that '[w]riting is not doomed to be the shadow of speech' (142). It is a measure of Coetzee's sleight of hand that he here assigns the role of postmodern speaker to the 'father of realism' (De)Foe, while he turns a metafictional character like Susan into a proponent of realism.

4.4 Part IV

In the final section, the instant the narration switches to the present tense, Susan and Foe lose their narrative voice to an unidentified first-person narrator, an 'authorial' voice supplying an ultimate frame to this metafiction. This narrator makes two attempts to make Friday's silence speak; in his second attempt, the novel 'makes its boldest metafictional gesture' (Head, 125). We encounter the narrator in a house identified as Daniel Defoe's, since it bears a commemorative plaque. There, the narrator heads for the box containing Susan's account of her island experiences. He begins to read the letter: 'Dear Mr Foe, At last I could row no further' (*F*, 155) – these are the words with which *Foe* opens and which the real reader has read at the beginning of the novel; one can recognise in this a mise-en-abyme of the reading process, rounding off the text.[21]

From here the desire of the multiple 'I', the 'merged' narratorial voices of Susan and the new narrator[22], to release Friday's story takes them to the wrecked ship, 'the home of Friday', a place beyond words, 'where bodies are their own signs' (*F*, 157). To 'make Friday's silence speak, as well as the silence surrounding Friday' (*F*, 142) has been discussed by the characters in the novel before, thus anticipating the culminating 'event' in the novel's final metafictional

---

[20] Cf. *F*, 152
[21] Cf. Engélibert, 276
[22] Cf. Attridge, 83

13

frame.[23] The diver, overcoming the taboo on mutilation, touches Friday, releasing a wordless, endless stream emanating from his mouth. Friday's very symbol of subjection, his tongueless silence, can then be seen as a means to undermine that subjection by usurping the story and overwhelming the narration in the closing lines:

> From inside him comes a slow stream, without breath, without interruption. It flows up through is body and out upon me; it passes through the cabin, through the wreck; washing the cliffs and shores of the island, it runs northward and southward to the ends of the earth. Soft and cold, dark and unending, it beats against my eyelids, against the skin of my face. (*F*, 157)

The novel's self-reflexivity finally leads to the 'self-canceling' of the 'self-representation' (Attwell, *Coetzee*, 114) of the authorial voice, standing for Coetzee's recognition of the 'limits [...] of the textual authority' (Attwell, *Coetzee*, 103) of the author: it is Coetzee refusing to write for Friday, hoping to be eventually silenced in favour of a black story.

---

[23] Cf. Head, 124

5. Conclusion

This paper has pointed out key metafictional instances, such as the characters recurrent reflections on their 'insubstantiality'[24], in Coetzee's *Foe* – a novel which, in spite of its relative shortness, has inspired a wealth of interpretations. It has also attempted to describe Coetzee's position in contemporary writing, and especially the difficulties in doing so. There are many areas which could have been covered in greater detail (for instance, the political issues raised by Coetzee's works, or his wide-ranging academic writing), but the scope of this paper would not have allowed it.

Being confident in the idea that 'narrative has the power to liberate the victims of our society', and to 'call those of us who read and write it to confession, and in confession there is hope for change' (Ledbetter, x), postcolonial writing has a crucial transformative function, both towards the works of the past and their potential role in the shaping of the future.

---

[24] Cf. Attridge, 74

Bibliography

Primary Literature

Coetzee, John Maxwell. *Foe*. Harmondsworth: Penguin, 1987.

Secondary Literature

Attridge, Derek. *J. M. Coetzee and the Ethics of Reading*. Chicago: University of Chicago Press, 2004.

Attwell, David. *J.M. Coetzee: South Africa and the Politics of Writing*. Berkeley: University of California Press, 1993.

Burnett, Paula. "The Ulyssean Crusoe and the Quest for Redemption in J.M. Coetzee's *Foe* and Derek Walcott's *Omeros*". *Robinson Crusoe. Myths and Metamorphoses*. Ed. Lieve Spaas and Brian Stimpson. London: Macmillan Press, 1996. 239-255.

Coetzee, J.M. and Attwell, D. (ed.). *Doubling The Point: Essays and Interviews*. Massachusetts: Harvard University Press, 1992.

Corcoran, Patrick. "*Foe*: Metafiction and the Discourse of Power". *Robinson Crusoe. Myths and Metamorphoses*. Ed. Lieve Spaas and Brian Stimpson. London: Macmillan Press, 1996. 256-266.

Derrida, Jacques. *Positions*. London: Athlone, 1981.

Derrida, Jacques. *Margins of Philosophy*. Chicago: University of Chicago Press, 1982.

Egerer, Claudia. "*Fictions of (In)Betweenness*". Diss. U of Göteborg, 1996.

Engélibert, Jean-Paul. "Daniel Defoe as Character: Subversions of the Myths of Robinson Crusoe and of the Author". *Robinson Crusoe. Myths and Metamorphoses*. Ed. Lieve Spaas and Brian Stimpson. London: Macmillan Press, 1996. 267-281.

Federman, Raymond. 1975. "Surfiction - Four Propositions in Form of an Introduction."
   Surfiction: Fiction Now and Tomorrow. Ed. Raymond Federman. Chicago: Swallow
   Press, 1981. 5-15.

Gallagher, Susan VanZanten. *A Story of South Africa: J. M. Coetzee's Fiction in Context.*
   Cambridge, Mass.: Harvard University Press, 1991.

Gass, William H. *Fiction and the Figures of Life*. New York: Knopf, 1970.

Head, Dominic: *J. M. Coetzee*. Cambridge: Cambridge University Press, 1997.

Hjelmslev, Louis. *Prolegomena to a Theory of Language*. Madison: Wisconsin, 1961.

Hutcheon, Linda. *Narcissistic Narrative. The Metafictional Paradox*. Wilfrid Laurier
   University Press, 1983.

James, Louis. "Retrospective and Prospective Views". *Robinson Crusoe. Myths and
   Metamorphoses*. Ed. Lieve Spaas and Brian Stimpson. London: Macmillan Press,
   1996. 1-9

Ledbetter, Mark. *Victims and the Postmodern Narrative, or Doing Violence to the Body: an
   Ethic of Reading and Writing*. Basingstoke: Macmillan, 1996.

Lyotard, Jean-Francois. *The Postmodern Condition: A Report on Knowledge*. Trans. Geoff
   Bennington and Brian Massumi. Minneapolis: University of Minnesota Press, 1984.

McCaffery, Larry. *The Metafictional Muse: the Works of Robert Coover, Donald Barthelme
   and William H. Gass.* Pittsburgh: University of Pittsburgh Press, 1982

Newman, Judie. *The Ballistic Bard: Postcolonial Fictions*. London: Arnold, 1995.

Ommundsen, Wenche. *Metafictions? Reflexivity in Contemporary Texts*. Australia:
   Melbourne UP, 1993.

Quendler, Christian. *From Romantic Irony to Postmodernist Metafiction: A Contribution to*

the History of Literary Self-Reflexivity in its Philosophical Context. Frankfurt am
Main: Lang, 2001.

Scott, Steven D. *The Gamefulness of American Postmodernism.* New York: Lang, 2000.

Splendore, Paola. "J. M. Coetzee's Foe: Intertextual and Metafictional Resonances."
Commonwealth: Essays and Studies 11.1 (1988): 55-60.

Waugh, Patricia. *Metafiction: The Theory and Practice of Self-Conscious Fiction.* London:
Routledge, 1990.

Wolf, Werner. *Ästhetische Illusion und Illusionsdurchbrechung in der Erzählkunst: Theorie
und Geschichte mit Schwerpunkt auf englischem illusionstörenden Erzählen.*
Tübingen: Niemeyer, 1993.

Yeoh, Gilbert Guan-Hin. "*The Persistence of Ethics: Ethical Readings of Samuel Beckett,
Primo Levi and J.M. Coetzee.*" Diploma Thesis Harvard University, 1998.

Books and articles not available

Begam, Richard. "Silence and Mut(e)ilation: White Writing in J. M. Coetzee's Foe." *South Atlantic Quarterly* 93.1 (1994): 111-129.

Clayton, Cherry. "White Writing and the Postcolonial Politics." *Ariel* 25.4 (1994): 153-167.

Olsen, Lance. "The Presence of Absence: Coetzee's *Waiting for the Barbarians*." *Ariel* 16.2 (1985): 47-56.

Wright, Derek. "Fiction as Foe: The Novels of J. M. Coetzee." *The International Fiction Review* 16.2 (1989): 113-18.